TEACHINGS OF BUDDHA

OTHER TITLES IN THIS SERIES

TEACHINGS OF HINDUISM

TEACHINGS OF MOHAMMAD

TEACHINGS OF JESUS CHRIST

In memory of Smt Maya Majumdar
— whose dreamchild this was!

TEACHINGS OF BUDDHA

AJANTA CHAKRAVARTY

RIDER

LONDON · SYDNEY · AUCKLAND · JOHANNESBURG

1 3 5 7 9 10 8 6 4 2

First published in 1997 by Shishti Publishers, India.
This edition published in 1998 by Rider, an imprint of
Ebury Press
Random House UK Ltd
Random House
20 Vauxhall Bridge Road
London SW1V 2SA

Random House Australia (Pty) Ltd
20 Alfred Street
Milsons Point, Sydney
New South Wales, 2016 Australia

Random House New Zealand Limited
18 Poland Road, Glenfield
Auckland 10, New Zealand

Random House South Africa (Pty) Limited
Endulini, 5A Jubilee Road
Parktown 2193, South Africa

Random House UK Limited Reg. No. 954009

Papers used by Rider Books are natural, recyclable products made from wood grown in sustainable forests.

Printed and bound in Great Britain by CPD, Wales

A CIP catalogue record for this book is available from the British Library

ISBN 0-7126-7177-3

Preface

The origin of life on earth is a contentious issue between scientists and believers. Scientists search for the truth, trying to prove its existence through rigorous experimentation, leaving no room for ambiguities. Believers, on the other hand take the existence of the Supreme Truth as granted; the rest follows thereafter with irrefutable logic.

What is generally overlooked is that between these conflicting views, there is a definite common factor about the beginning of life, the coming into existence of living matter. This is the manifestation of the 'life-force' or what has been described by many as the 'vital elan'. This force must have a 'life space' around it to provide for its sustenance and reproduction. The two must fit precisely and harmoniously for life to grow, flourish and evolve into its many different forms.

There were calamities too. The iceage, the submergences, earthquakes, tornadoes, avalanches, and the volcanic eruptions changed life space so dramatically that entire species were wiped out. There were other disasters, less dramatic but of no less magnitude. Exhaustion of natural food resources, spoiling of natural habitat, and overcrowding of life space led to large-scale disasters. The changes in environment meant that the vital elan had two options, either to adapt to the changes or be annihilated. Very often it was the latter because the species lacked the ability to adjust to the oncoming changes and reorient themselves until it was too late.

When man finally appeared on earth, he was as exposed to all the vagaries of life space as other species. But he was intelligent. He could observe, reason, deduce and apply the core of his thinking to harness the life space rather than be driven by it. He searched actively for means of enhancing the 'vital elan' and his quest was both in the physical world outside and the spiritual world within himself. The last gave rise to religion.

It is often thought that primordial man was a not-so-clever animal, who blindly worshipped the forces of nature – the rocks, trees, streams, clouds and the stars. Many have expressed doubts about organized religion on account of its being an atavistic throwback to the dark ages of the past. In today's world of fast-paced determinism, religion is often publicly scorned but privately engaged in to propitiate the very same forces that may in some way make life space more acceptable to us. And in this cauldron of conflicting desires and ambitions, the true significance of religion and the religious teachings and precepts get lost.

Man's search for tools with which to master his environment led to science. But prior to that, he had evolved language, without which no development would have been possible. Language gave him the means to communicate his thoughts, his feelings, his enquiries with others. His superior brain enabled the processing of loose, unstructured information into systematic forms. This was knowledge, the most powerful tool at his command. He could use it for harmony, growth and peace or for wanton annihilation. What he needed were guidelines for implementing his knowledge. He sought the power of wisdom. And once again, he turned, both to the forces outside to understand the mysteries of nature and within, to know the truth of his very being. He wanted to learn from the Masters who had drunk deep of the springs of wisdom and on whose teachings were founded the great religions, the pathways of discernment.

It must be noted that many religions have come into being and almost as many have disappeared without trace. They could not measure up to the changing demands of life space. Those which survived went through many trials and tribulations, each tempering its core values for greater robustness. Their Masters, often coming at the darkest hour, brought messages of hope. Of good sense. Of homespun, sensible practices which could be adopted by all, irrespective of birth and position. Unfortunately, the passage of time invariably obscured these precepts. The primary cause for this was that the language forms underwent spatial and temporal changes, restructuring and reinterpreting. These variations proceeded to filter into common usage according to their ability of easing Man's understanding. Over time, the regular languages changed their forms so radically that the scriptural languages were rendered impotent. Thus the wisdom inherent in them was lost to new generations.

This series of books attempts to rediscover and reinterpret some of the teachings from the scriptures of a few mainstream religions, in a form suitable for absorption by the twentieth century person poised on the threshold of the twenty-first. The kind of world we will make then will depend to a great extent on the wisdom that precedes every small or big decision. Perhaps the information in this book will help in reinforcing the learning for making a better and more beautiful life space for humanity at large.

TEACHINGS OF BUDDHA

Gautama Buddha was the only son of his parents King Shuddodhana and Queen Mayadevi of Kapilavastu. Legend has it that one night Mayadevi dreamt of a pure white elephant that descended from heaven and entered her womb. Soon afterwards she found that she was with child. Later at an advanced stage of pregnancy, as she travelled through the Lumbini forests on her way home the labour pains began. She was clutching the bough of a banyan tree with raised arms when Gautama came into the world. This nativity scene is the subject of many a Buddhist painting.

Gautama's childhood name was Siddhartha. A wise man on seeing the child prophesied, 'This child will bring deliverance to the whole world. Though he will never be a king, he will be known as the King of Kings.'

His apprehensive parents virtually imprisoned him in a

pleasure garden where no sorrow of any kind was allowed to enter. At a fairly early age Siddhartha was married to a beautiful Princess Yashodhara. In due course, a son Rahul was born to them.

One day Siddhartha managed to slip out of the palace in his chariot. In the course of his perambulations, he came across a sick person, an old man and a dead body being taken for cremation. There was much sorrow around all three. Finally he saw a sanyasi who appeared to be ensconsed in a field of ineffable joy. What he saw gave him food for much thought. He decided to renounce the world in search of the one great unalterable truth. One night, he silently left all his relatives and worldly possessions to go into self exile.

Most of his meditations were at Uruvilva which is now known as Bodh-Gaya. After six years of constant endeavour, the much desired enlightenment dawned on him. He began to preach the new gospel and his followers lovingly called him Bodhisattva, one who knows the truth.

The first sermon was preached at Sarnath near Varanasi. For forty-five years, the Buddha continued his mission with unabated zeal. His followers were organized into well structured sanghas so that the message may continue to spread through systematic pathways. On the night of Vaishakh Purnima, Buddha entered into the Great Silence (Maha Nirvana) at Kushinara. He was then eighty years old. This day is said to be thrice blessed as on this day Buddha was born, attained enlightenment and breathed his last.

Buddha's life was an example of immense sacrifice and immaculate purity. His teachings left an indelible imprint on the traditional, and to a certain extent ritual-bound Hinduism of that period. His words gave life to many of the basic precepts of the Vedas that had become obscure with time. He taught compassion, forgiveness and truth to be the greatest virtues. Swami Vivekanand had described him as the 'Ultimate Karmayogi of the Upanishads'. Even today, his life and teachings influence the daily lives and aspirations of millions.

Buddhists chronicle the reincarnations of Buddha in the Jatakas. These precepts have been drawn from them and other Buddhist literature.

If you take care of each other, you will take care of all mankind.

If tomorrow is uncertain, why do you delay your good deeds for it?

Every mistake carries an inherent lesson.

Who is the greater enemy ... the man outside or your evil thoughts within?

Do every man the honour of listening to him.

Words can burn. Words can soothe. Use them wisely.

If you sow hatred, can you reap compassion?

Anger and jealousy are boulders in the fountain of natural goodness.

Was hatred ever snuffed out by hatred? It can only be extinguished by love.

It is said that life is the most precious possession. Yet it is the most uncertain.

Follow the middle path. Neither extreme will make you happy.

Each one of us sees the world through the window of his thoughts.

The more we give, the more we get.

Is not hope a wonderful thing? It keeps us going from day to day.

In the travel through life, some gather wisdom, some gather stones, some gather nothing.

Desire does not create problems. Our attachments to desire do.

Be honourable in your actions, sincere in your speech. Do not worry about what others think about you.

A man who knows the way but does not practise it is like the miser who keeps a king's treasure under lock and key.

The humble ant shows us how to work; the bee how to live in harmony.

There is no greater gift than good health. Take care of it.

Can he who is not at peace himself bring peace unto others?

No good is higher than truth and compassion.

Wisdom is the lamp, good thoughts the oil, sweet words the flame.

Sit quietly and listen to the voice of your mind. Do you like the words it speaks?

Share your food with others as the mother does with her children.

Let go of your petty desires. Experience the joy of freedom.

The only things death cannot erase are our good deeds.

Shed your past like a snake sheds its skin.

Enjoy yourself wherever you are, do not crave to be where others may be.

A wise man does not fear death.

You stand at the crossroads of the path of love and the path of fear. Which do you choose to follow?

Why do you shun the carcass? It provides fertiliser for your fields.

When anger blinds you, ask how wise men would behave under similar circumstances?

Do not ask the world to change. Change yourself.

A life of simplicity and love is one of peace.

Neither judge yourself nor others. Learn from mistakes.

Let a poor man live wisely. Let a rich man live wisely.

Give your thoughts a chance to settle down. Then feel your mind clear like a still forest pool.

Love for all washes your mind clean.

Truth is inside you. To see it you must open the inner eye.

Once you have seen the truth, you are happy for all eternity.

Give generously. Feel the power of generosity.

Are you ruled by your own values or by
others' opinions?

One who can turn conflict into collaboration is the Buddha.

Be calm, like a great tree in a storm.

Nothing harms more than perfidy.

Forgive the action, forget the intent.

There are many ways in which you can be hurt. But there is only one way to heal. That is through love.

Can one who does not feel another's agony be compassionate?

Do not scorn the old and the wretched. You too are subject to decay.

Do not shudder at the sight of an afflicted person. You too may be subject to disease.

To disrespect your father is wrong. To despise him is a sin.

Why starve your body or overstuff it like a glutton? Follow the middle path.

No mortal act can cleanse a man who deliberately wears the chains of delusion.

To light the Soul-fire, make your body sound and healthy.

Evil intentions cause uncleanliness, not the lack of a bath or washed clothing.

All mortification is valueless if the self lusts after earthly or heavenly pleasures.

To satisfy the necessities of life is not evil.

Stand together so that a weak man may avail of your strength to walk the right path.

Seek the welfare of men but look not for recompense, not even to be born in heaven.

A single sentence that pacifies the distressed is better than thousands of lectures.

Meditate on pity so that you develop deep compassion for all beings in distress.

Meditate on love so that you long for the welfare of all, even your enemies.

Meditate on impurity when you consider the consequences of corruption, both physical and mental.

Meditate on joy so that you can rejoice at the prosperity of others.

Meditate on serenity when you can contemplate your own fate with impartial calmness and perfect tranquility.

The path is for anyone who can destroy craving.

A paranoid man destroys himself more than others.

An ill-directed mind will cause greater harm to a person than his enemy.

One who is awake need not fear nightmares of delusion.

By oneself is one purified. No one can purify another.

By oneself alone is evil done. Do not seek to transfer the responsibility of your wrong deeds.

The world may see a corrupt man living in luxury. That man alone knows the torments that keep him awake.

The evil of small lies should not be taken lightly. Even a water-jar is filled by the falling drops.

Look for goodness in your fellow beings so that you may defend them to their enemies with sincerity.

If a man commits a sin, let him not do it again.

The spirit of Buddha is in sublime forbearance and patience.

The preacher must not carp at others or blame other preachers.

The preacher must not mention by name those whom they want to reproach publicly.

Why blame fate for the sorrows in our lives?
We make them with our own actions.

Wherever you go, spread the perfume of happiness.

True happiness is not built on the sorrows of another.

Truth is not with the preacher. It is in your heart. The preacher opens a window to it.

If you want to add value to your entire life,
take care of every moment.

Your forgiveness should not become your weakness. Do not allow the same injustice a second time.

Use your strength to help the weak, not humiliate the poor.

Do you seek miracles in temples? Try seeing them in the humble flowers growing unbidden at your doorstep.

Look for happiness in simple things.
Complexities create problems.

Meditation thrives on a kind and happy heart.

Forgive from the heart, not just with the tongue.

What good is the knowledge that does not bring wisdom?

The more we possess, the more we want.

Learn to let go and be free.

Kindness should become the natural way of life, not the exception.

Experiences should be our guide. Let them not enslave us.

Remembering a wrong is like carrying a burden on the mind.

Learn to forgive and be free.

Life is rich with possibilities of action. The enlightened choose carefully.

Be aware of your inner tranquility as you sail
the rough seas of your life.

When you count what others have, also count what you have that others do not.

Every morning is a new beginning.